# PASSPORTS TO PEACE

# PASSPORTS TO PEACE

## Embassies and the Art of Diplomacy

**Nancy Warren Ferrell**

Lerner Publications Company · Minneapolis

**The author wishes to thank Barnett B. Lester, Associate Editor, *State* Magazine, for his help, cooperation, and advice during the preparation of this book.**

Thanks also to the many United States agencies and foreign embassies who contributed information or illustrative materials to this book. More personally, special thanks to Thomas M. Tracy, U.S. Assistant Secretary of State for Administration; Anne Symington of the Cultural Section of the U.S. Embassy, London, England; and John H. Dieffenderfer, Administrative Officer, the U.S. Embassy, Dublin, Ireland.

The quotes on the following pages are used with permission:

Page 32 from "A Short History of the U.S. Department of State, 1781-1981," published by the U.S. Department of State, January 1981.

Page 64 from "Careers: Joining the Foreign Service," Nancy J. White, *Working Woman,* October, 1981.

The chart on pp. 18-19 has been reprinted from "The Department of State Today," published by the U.S. Department of State, March 1984.

Photo credits: Wide World Photos, pp. 20 & 23; *State* Magazine, pp. 13, 51, 55, 76, 77, & 82; United Nations, pp. 33 & 68.



Manufactured in the United States of America

Library of Congress Cataloging-in-Publication Data



**Ferrell, Nancy Warren.**
Passports to peace.

Includes index.
Summary: An overview of the world of diplomacy, including its history and kinds of jobs in the foreign service.
1. Diplomacy—Juvenile literature. 2. Diplomatic and consular service—Juvenile literature. [1. Diplomacy] I. Title.
JX1664.F47 1985 327.2 85-16006
ISBN 0-8225-0644-0 (lib. bdg.)

2 3 4 5 6 7 8 9 10 94 93 92 91 90 89 88 87 86

*To my brother, Tom Warren,*
*who took the longest trip too soon*

# Contents

# 1
# What Is Diplomacy?

Everyone who travels to a foreign country or who meets a foreign visitor in his or her own country is a kind of **diplomat**. The foreign visitor might be a tourist who asks you for directions on the street or an exchange student who has come to live for a year in your town. How each of us acts toward foreigners and how they behave toward us helps shape the opinion each will hold of the other's country.

Official diplomats are those people who have been appointed to represent their country's government in other nations or international organizations. Their home away from home is the **diplomatic mission**, or **embassy**. An **ambassador** is a diplomat who has been chosen to head an embassy or a mission.

All countries of the world send diplomats to friendly nations. Working among other people, these diplomats create a base for greater understanding between countries. In this way, embassies become tools for peace.

**Diplomacy**, in simple terms, is the art of handling affairs, whether personal or political, without fighting. Most people practice diplomacy daily without even realizing it. At school, taking turns is a diplomatic solution to the problem of who goes first. At home, parents and children use diplomacy when they negotiate such things as use of the family car. Whether between two people or two nations, diplomacy works in the same way. Differences of opinion are discussed and negotiated. Diplomacy has prevented many wars, while other wars have occurred despite great efforts on the part of many diplomats.

Just as people are different because of the way in which they have been raised, so too are countries different. In each country, language, geography, resources, history, and government all play a part in shaping that country.

Diplomacy, therefore, requires a willingness to learn about other cultures and ways of life. By living in another country, diplomats can begin to understand the values and needs of the people in that country and can help to find peaceful solutions to difficult problems.

# 2
# How Diplomatic Missions Work

Nations send representatives to friendly capitals in the world for two reasons: to protect their own interests and to learn more about the other country and its people.

## Embassies

The main purpose of an embassy is to speak and act for its government. The Russian embassy, for instance, reports that its function is to "represent its country abroad, within the territorial jurisdiction of another country...with the primary purpose of maintaining official contacts between the governments of the two countries."

Diplomats who live in other countries are in a better position to understand the feelings of the people and the policies of the government there. Those interests can then be communicated to the home nation.

In each country, foreign governments can establish only one embassy. Small or not yet well-established nations, such as Djibouti, a tiny country on Africa's northeastern coast, cannot afford embassies all over the world. Instead, they send one **delegation**, or group, of diplomats, headed by an ambassador, to the United Nations to conduct business with the representatives of many countries.

Some nations, although they could afford it, do not have embassies in certain countries, either for political reasons or for reasons of safety. The United States, for instance, does not operate an embassy in Cuba because of U.S. national policy and no longer has an embassy in Iran because of the danger there.

Of all the American embassies, the Tokyo mission is the largest. It is followed in size by those in Paris, London, New Delhi, Mexico City, and Bonn. Each post supports a different number of employees. The U.S. Embassy in London operates with 600 workers—half are American citizens, and half are citizens of the United Kingdom.

The everyday work of diplomacy is performed in the **chancery**, or offices, of the embassy. Imagine you are visiting the American embassy in Dublin, Ireland. You stand in front of a modern circular structure that suggests monuments of centuries past. The building is surrounded by a "moat" of shrubbery. If you were to step through its front doors, you would first face a glassed-in security office. There marines and other personnel would ask you whom you wished to visit and whether you had an appointment. They might answer your questions or direct you to the proper department. If you had a camera, the guards would take it from you so that you could not take photographs inside the building and return it when you were ready to leave the building.

When you stepped past the guards, you would be in a large, round lobby in the center of the building, surrounded by offices. And if you toured the building, you would find more offices upstairs and downstairs.

A large American chancery has several departments.

**The U.S. embassy in Dublin**

One department in the embassy is responsible for writing news items for the local press, while others schedule cultural tours, help the Peace Corps, arrange for security, report on political meetings, keep the embassy budget in balance, and assist tourists who lose their passports.

Embassy staff is composed of people who make a career out of working in foreign countries. Additional staff members are citizens of the host country and work in almost every department in the embassy. Their presence adds continuity to the embassy's work as foreign service officers leave for other assignments and new foreign service workers come in to take their places. In countries where the language is different, embassies also employ translators.

Just as a nation has only one embassy in another country, it has only one ambassador there. The ambassador, also called the **chief of mission**, is the director of the embassy. He or she is assisted by a **deputy chief of mission**. Before an ambassador can take over a new post, he or she must be approved by the host country. Most of the time, this process is simply a formality.

In most nations, an ambassador is promoted to his or her post after many years of foreign service work. He or she is called a "career diplomat" because official diplomacy is his or her life's work. One such career diplomat is George Kennan. Mr. Kennan joined the foreign service in 1926 and rose up through the ranks. He was eventually assigned first as ambassador to Russia (1952) and later as ambassador to Yugoslavia (1961). He is now a Professor Emeritus at Princeton University.

In the United States, there is another way to become an ambassador. The president of the United States can appoint an ambassador, even though the person to be appointed has had no previous foreign service experience. John Louis, Jr., former U.S. ambassador to the United Kingdom, was an appointee without foreign service experience. He was, however, a well-educated, well-traveled person with previous experience in international business relations.

Both methods of becoming an ambassador have their advantages. A career diplomat brings experience to the ambassador's job that an appointee does not have. But some people, on the other hand, believe that ambassadorial posts should be filled with "outside" diplomats—people outside the foreign service who bring other experience to the job.

Whether a career diplomat or an appointed one, an ideal ambassador must be honest, cautious, educated, and courageous. He or she must have traveled and must possess political sense and skill. Also, since budgets are limited and entertaining expenses substantial, it helps if an ambassador is wealthy. After all, some expenses may well come out of the ambassador's personal pocket.

The ambassador's full title is *ambassador extraordinary and plenipotentiary*, or just E. and P. The extra tag signifies that the ambassador has powers to negotiate ordinary diplomatic problems. If something as important as a treaty has to be signed, however, the U.S. ambassador must receive special permission from the president and Congress.

Many of an ambassador's duties require listening and talking. An American ambassador, for instance, meets with business and political officials of the host country, discusses the problems of that country, and explains American policies to them, all while keeping the president and the secretary of state informed. The ambassador also entertains those officials at teas and receptions as well as hosting American business people and politicians who are traveling abroad.

A typical day for a United States ambassador might go something like this: After traveling to a nearby city, the ambassador spends the morning visiting a factory and talking with the workers. The ambassador makes a speech at the country's civil service office, eats lunch, and then lectures at a university. Next the ambassador visits the construction site of a dam, and then heads home to prepare for a formal dinner in the evening.

The U.S. diplomat who ranks next to an ambassador in power is a **minister**. Years ago, ministers headed **legations**, which are like embassies but much smaller. Since 1966, however, U.S. missions have all become embassies, and legations are no longer being established. **Envoy** is a general term used to describe an ambassador or a minister.

Other high-ranking diplomats include the **chargé d'affaires**, who takes over when the ambassador or minister is not present. Chargé d'affaires L. Bruce Laingen was ranking officer at the U.S. embassy in

Teheran, Iran, during the hostage ordeal in 1979.

The representatives of the U.S. government agencies and the foreign service officers at a foreign mission are generally called the "country team." In all cases, offices are staffed with competent deputies, secretaries, attachés, officers, stenographers, receptionists, assistants, military personnel, and translators. Each person works hard to support the chief of mission in his or her diplomatic duties.

## Consulates

In large countries, a government might have **consulates** as well as an embassy. While the embassy deals with political issues, a consulate deals mostly with private citizens and commercial business. It handles such commercial activities in the host country as fishing problems, oil interests, and tourists' complaints. In Spain, for instance, the United States has an embassy in Madrid and consulates in Barcelona, Seville, and Bilbao.

All told, the United States operates more than 140 embassies throughout the world, with over 100 additional consulates. In countries that do not have separate consulates, there is usually a consular department within the embassy to handle these commercial affairs.

Strictly speaking, consulates are diplomatic only in part, since they are concerned mostly with commercial business. Yet many of the rules that apply to embassies and ambassadors apply also to consulates and **consuls**, those officials appointed to staff a consulate.

The head of a consulate, called a **consul general**, must be approved by the host country just as an ambassador is approved. The consular corps has a distinct diplomatic flavor because its members are constantly coming into contact with important information. The consuls are always aware of national developments, some of which might later develop into important diplomatic affairs.

At certain times, the consul may find himself in the

---

## A U.S. Mission in a Foreign Country

This chart shows the U.S. embassy in Venezuela. Besides the 112 Americans employed in Caracas when this chart was drawn up, there were 4 Americans on staff at the U.S. Consulate in Maracaibo, Venezuela. There were additional civilian and military employees of the Department of Defense. Also present were employees of the Federal Aviation Administration, on hand to carry out a short-term assignment.

| | | | | | |
|---|---|---|---|---|---|
| Mission Unit | Agricultural Trade Office | Agricultural Counselor | Public Affairs Counselor | Commercial Counselor | Political Counselor |
| Home Agency | Agriculture | Agriculture | USIA | Commerce | |

position of being the only diplomat in a country or the most available diplomat. One notable example is Park Wollam, the U.S. consul who arranged to free captive Americans in Cuba in the late 1950s. With risk to his own life, the consul talked rebel Cuban guerrillas into releasing the hostages. Fortunately, a consul's work is not often concerned with such dire life-and-death situations.

While traveling, the individual citizen will be more likely to use the services of the consular department of an embassy than any other department. It is the consular department and the consulate that grant

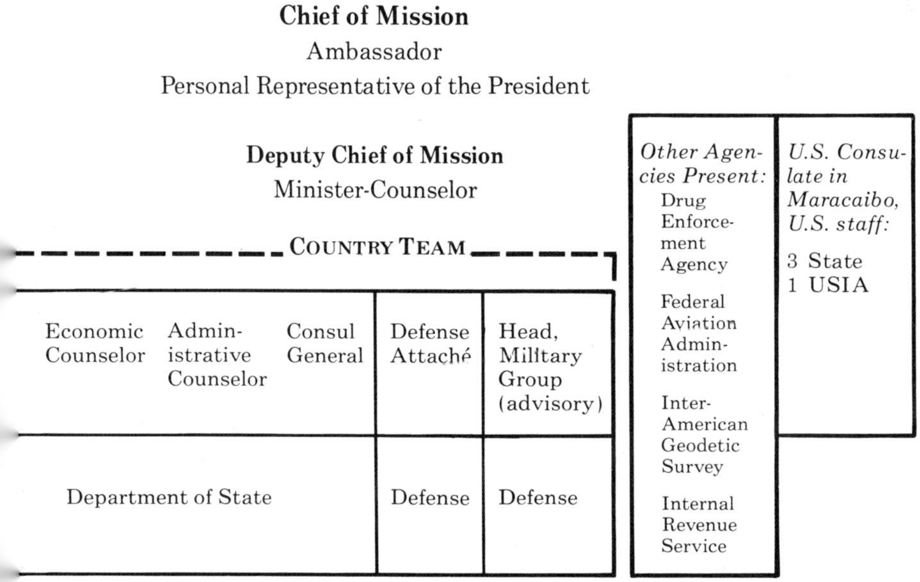

travel visas. Consulates also advise traveling business people of potential markets for their products within the host country.

But it is the traveling tourist who finds a consular face most appealing. When the traveler has lost his or her passport or becomes sick, when a relative has passed away on the trip, when a father wants to visit a son in jail—these are all times when the consul steps in to help. Consular officers smooth out the rough spots between citizens and foreign authorities.

## Security

Security has always been a concern for embassies, but never as great a concern as it is today. Up until the mid-1960s, the safety of diplomats was almost always honored. Since that time, however, embassies and diplomats have been the target of terrorist groups or mobs. If the people of a nation disagree with what another country is doing, they often take their protest directly to that country's embassy. Terrorists can storm missions, take over, and hold hostages, just as the Iranians did in Teheran.

It was February 14, 1979, when frenzied mobs ran through the streets of Teheran. Religious followers under the leadership of Ayatollah Ruhollah Khomeini were overthrowing the Shah, the ruler of Iran. Street

**Demonstrators were shouting anti-American slogans outside the U.S. embassy in Tehran, while inside fifty-two Americans were being held hostage.**

الله اکبر

gangs armed with G3 rifles and pistols roamed the buildings and alleyways of the capital. Few knew who was who or to what faction anyone belonged. Finally, the free-form chaos focused on the U.S. embassy. The 150 attackers sprayed rifle fire into the embassy compound, broke through the gates and into the building, and held 102 Americans hostage. Later on the same day, the Iranian army arranged for a cease-fire, and the embassy seige was over.

But this Teheran trouble was only the prelude to the actual overthrow almost nine months later. In early November of the same year, Iranian mobs stormed the U.S. embassy once again, but this time took it over. For 444 days, fifty-two U.S. citizens were held hostage. They were finally released and sent home in January 1981.

Not all U.S. embassies and consulates require added security. The State Department pinpoints embassies that are located in potential trouble spots. Those embassies receive extra security in a manner termed "concentric circles of denial." The outer limits of this circle include the outside grounds area, the next ring includes the building, and the next includes the inside of the building. The core area is equipped with food, water, and other supplies so that a staff under attack can hold out until they are rescued.

Such tactics enabled 117 Americans to survive a mob assault in 1979 at the U.S. embassy in Islamabad, Pakistan. The staff retired to a communications vault

**The damaged U.S. embassy in Beirut: the car exploded before the driver could reach the underground garage.**

in the building until Pakistani troops—and darkness—discouraged the mob.

Holding strategies like these also allow time for the staff to destroy secret information rather than let it fall into unfriendly hands. While the State Department is trying to beef up security at its embassies around the world, it is also trying to keep the outside of these embassies looking fairly natural—not like military bunkers. Planning, building, and installing these changes can take up to three years.

Safety precautions did not arrive in time to save the U.S. embassy in Beirut, Lebanon. After a bombing attack on the U.S. embassy in West Beirut, the area

was considered too dangerous, and the entire embassy complex was moved to a safer spot, a suburban village in East Beirut. The entrance to the new location was studded with waist-high concrete cubes called "dragon's teeth." These were placed in the road so that a car could not be driven on a straight path but had to be maneuvered around the blocks, slowing it down considerably. Holes drilled into the concrete cubes were awaiting an iron gate, which was to be installed in a few days.

Before the gate went up, however, a car bearing what appeared to be Dutch diplomatic license plates and loaded with hundreds of pounds of explosives careened around the concrete blocks. Marines and guards fired on the vehicle, but by that time the car had passed through the barricade and exploded in front of the embassy. The force of the blast killed over thirty people. As a guard later stated, the car could not have entered had the outer gate been in position.

In addition to shoring up physical security at U.S. embassies, the State Department is also retraining embassy guards to combat terrorism. Marine guards have long been protectors of embassy grounds. In early diplomatic years, the United States employed civilians to guard embassies. Sometimes these civilians were Americans, and sometimes they were citizens of the host country. But these people were not trained in security work nor in some cases were they even suited for it. It was clear that a disciplined, alert military force was needed. The U.S. Marines were designated to perform this job.

All men in the Marine Security Guard Battalion are taken from regular marine ranks and attend special training at the Marine Security Guard school in Quantico, Virginia. The school covers such subjects as weapons training, terrorism, physical fitness, security procedures, and hostage training. In addition, the marines learn some of the rules of diplomacy.

Although marine guards are being trained to be a force against terrorists, they are not expected to fight a mob. Instead, their job is to fend off the enemy long enough for embassy personnel to reach safety and for the host government to react with help against such hostile attacks.

# 3
# The Growth of Diplomacy

Early world history is marked by wars, but it is also marked with attempts at peacemaking. As far back as the fifteenth century B.C., Egypt was trying to settle disputes with her neighbors in a peaceful manner. China, too, recognized merchants as information bearers and used them as **emissaries** for diplomatic missions—and sometimes for spying. As early as the thirteenth century B.C., the Chinese were negotiating with Japanese rulers.

## Fifth Century B.C.

The man Mo Tzu of China may not have been the first roaming diplomat, but he was certainly an interesting one. In the fifth century B.C., he and his followers, all believers in neighborly love, traveled on foot to different potential war sites to try to negotiate peace between the factions. If the two warring sides would not agree to settle their affairs without fighting, Mo Tzu and his followers joined the weaker side and trained them into stronger troops. When both sides were considered militarily equal, Mo Tzu then asked the leaders to sit down again and settle things peacefully.

## Early Greeks and Romans

Greece could well be considered the birthplace of diplomacy. Greek practices during the sixth century B.C. spawned terms used in diplomacy today; reconciliation, alliance, and convention are a few examples. The Greek nation was made up of small city-states. Often one city-state would send an emissary to a neighboring city on business. If a disagreement arose while he was there, the visitor would try to talk it out and achieve a peaceful solution. When an emissary returned home, he was judged on the effectiveness of his diplomatic work. If he had not done a good job, he might be thrown in jail or even killed. But it was a privilege to be an emissary, and the honor outweighed the risk.

Several centuries later, the Roman Empire developed the practice of sending emissaries to other countries. They even passed a law that ambassadors could travel safely without being bothered. In this way the practice of **immunity** evolved, an immunity that covered not only the ambassador but his attendants as well.

## The Middle Ages

With the growth of large powerful families in Italy after 1000 A.D., diplomacy took on a professional tone. Francesco Sforza, Duke of Milan, is credited with establishing the first permanent embassy in the fifteenth century A.D. He established it in Florence, Italy, at the court of the Medici, one of Italy's most powerful families. The Italians began to require written reports from their ambassadors in the field. To store these reports, diplomatic libraries were developed.

The growth of diplomacy was not without its problems, though. Some ambitious Italian families and Byzantine rulers began using ambassadors for business as well as political negotiations. Ambassadors soon developed a reputation for being liars and spies. Their words were met with suspicion. And although diplomats visited and enjoyed court life in their host country, they became more and more isolated from the common people. In some countries, a person even talking to an ambassador on the street might be suspected of being a spy. This attitude did not begin to change until the 1800s. At that time, French statesmen stressed the idea that diplomacy would be better served by practicing honesty instead of deception.

Yet another problem plagued diplomats: the ever-present dilemma of **precedence**. The solution to the "who would go first" question often depended on how fast the carriage of each diplomat could get him to the palace. Whose coach would go first in a parade, who would sit next to the king at dinner—these were but two of the many questions of rank. Since ambassadors represented their monarch in person, an insult to the diplomat was construed as an insult to his leader. His position in relation to others was very important.

## The Congress of Vienna

After Napoleon was defeated in Europe in 1812, the victorious nations called a peace convention. This gathering, known as the Congress of Vienna, convened during 1814 and 1815. Part of the resulting treaty dealt with diplomatic precedence.

The Congress determined the order of importance of diplomatic rank at official functions, naming ambassadors higher than ministers, for example. In addition, the Congress agreed that in cases of equal rank, the date of a diplomat's arrival in the country would determine his precedence. Thus, if a Spanish minister arrived in Canada at noon and an Australian minister arrived there just six hours later, the Spaniard would be given precedence over the Australian at all functions.

Though the precedence articles of the Congress were by no means law, all countries of the world continue to respect their basic guidelines, even today. Some Catholic countries, however, make an exception to this rule by automatically giving the Pope's emissary, called a **nuncio**, the highest rank.

Thanks to the Congress of Vienna and tradition, diplomatic standards were eventually set. Ambassadors shared freedom from restraint and immunity from the laws of the host nation. These privileges were also extended to encompass the residence and the family of the diplomat.

## U.S. Diplomacy

The United States was a latecomer to the field of diplomacy. After the nation became independent in 1776, only seven foreign countries were represented in the United States. Spain, the Netherlands, Great Britain, and France all sent ministers; Portugal and Prussia sent chargés d'affaires, and Denmark sent a consul who took over until a minister was assigned. By 1800, the foreign diplomatic corps in the U.S. numbered close to twenty members.

Washington, D.C. was considered a hardship post in the early days. The city lacked the polish of European courts, and it was a punishment to be sent there. Because Washington did not have enough housing, diplomats were forced to live in boarding houses. There were few good restaurants, and on top of everything else, it was unbearably hot during the summer. Only after the United States grew into a world power did diplomats' attitudes toward being posted there begin to change.

In 1781, Robert R. Livingston was selected by the new U.S. Congress as the first Secretary for Foreign Affairs. He operated out of a small brick house in Philadelphia, which was then still the nation's capitol. Not long after that, President George Washington appointed Thomas Jefferson as the first Secretary of State. The State Department handled embassies then, just as it does today.

Another well-known American, Benjamin Franklin, served as the first American minister overseas when he presented his credentials to the French court in 1779. The very nature of the new U.S. government, based on rule by the people rather than by royalty, presented difficulties. Dr. Franklin was an ordinary man who wore no court finery but dressed simply in business clothes of the day. His down-to-earth manner won him many friends, yet his manner of dress became a problem.

Royal families, used to jewels, braids, medals, frills, and pomp, were horrified by the way Ben Franklin and other American diplomats dressed. They looked like servants at court. When one American diplomat insisted on his plain clothes, Queen Victoria of England allowed him to wear a sword to distinguish him from the court workers.

By the beginning of the twentieth century, the U.S. had grown into an important nation in world affairs. The American foreign service overseas, which had numbered 62 members in 1800, totaled 1,137 by 1900. In turn, many more foreign governments had assigned representatives to Washington, D.C., which by then sported an impressive Embassy Row.

## Women in the Foreign Service

During the growth years, the U.S. Department of State hired women for clerical positions only. In 1905,

Assistant Secretary Frederick Van Dyne gave one reason: "The greatest obstacle to the employment of women as diplomatic agents is their well-known inability to keep a secret."

The first woman to step out of the clerical ranks and into a supervisory position was Margaret Hanna. She was hired in 1895 and spent many years as a clerk before she finally achieved the position of Chief of the Correspondence Bureau in 1918. Fifteen years later, Ruth Bryan Owen was named to the first top post as Minister to Denmark. She had no previous foreign service experience.

It was not until well after the Second World War, though, that a woman achieved ambassadorial rank. In 1953, Frances E. Willis took that honor when she was appointed ambassador to Switzerland.

## The United Nations

Both World War I and World War II made it plain that the world was growing smaller. The emergence of telegraph and cable facilities, radio, and airline travel all allowed diplomats faster access to their own leaders as well as to diplomats of other countries.

The experience of World War II also made several nations vow to prevent such a war from ever happening again. Representatives of those nations met to plan a peace-keeping organization. Out of these talks came

**United Nations headquarters in New York City**

the United Nations, formed in 1945 with 50 nations. Since that time, over 100 more countries have achieved independence and joined the U.N.

The United Nations provides a place where independent states of the world can meet to discuss world problems and to work out solutions to conflicts between countries. Just as governments send ambassadors to foreign countries, they also send diplomats to the United Nations. Many countries consider the U.N. a permanent mission, much like an embassy itself. Indeed, some small nations cannot afford an extensive network of embassies and concentrate their efforts at the U.N.

Not all members of the U.N. are ambassadors, but many have that rank. Though U.S. laws apply there, the actual site is owned by the United Nations and is considered international land. Representatives to the U.N. enjoy the same privileges and immunities as their fellow diplomats in other countries.

Each fall, all the delegates to the United Nations meet at the U.N. General Assembly. Committees formed by the General Assembly work on specific issues throughout the year. To carry out its duties, the United States retains five ambassadors at the U.N. in New York. In addition, the United States has special U.N. ambassadors in Geneva, Vienna, Washington, and Brussels, and two in Paris. In each of these locations is an international U.N. agency devoted to one specific cause.

# 4 The Privileges of Diplomacy

Diplomats are given immunity, or freedom, from local laws in their host countries. If an Italian diplomat breaks a law in Spain, for instance, the Spanish authorities cannot arrest him. The Spanish diplomat living in Italy has the same protection. The laws of immunity are not designed to allow diplomats to commit crimes in their host countries, but rather to protect them should they unknowingly break a law. Diplomats cannot be taxed, sued, or prosecuted in any way.

The rules of diplomatic immunity were not recognized until 1708. It was then that a Russian diplomat living in London was badly beaten by merchants for not paying his bills. After this incident, an act was passed to protect foreign diplomats from local pressures. Diplomats who abuse these privileges are likely to be removed from their posts by their own governments.

In the 1950s, the U.S. State Department began to issue identification cards to foreign diplomats. This card announces a diplomat's immunity. Before these cards were issued, a car carrying an Iranian minister was stopped by a highway patrolman in Maryland. Unfamiliar with the laws of immunity, the patrolman paid no attention to the Iranian's protest and arrested him. He had heard of Baptist ministers, the officer said, but never of Iranian ministers. The Iranian diplomat was later freed with many apologies, but it almost caused an international incident.

Besides immunity, another privilege enjoyed by diplomats and their families is the **right to chapel**. This right allows diplomats to practice their own religion on embassy grounds, whether or not the country in which it is situated has a national religion. Such was the case of Lord Chilston, a British ambassador and a Catholic. In Russia, where the government does not believe in religion, Lord Chilston arranged for and was allowed his own chaplain in the British embassy during the 1930s.

Freedom from taxation is probably the most prized personal privilege of diplomats. They are allowed to bring duty-free items into a foreign country without paying tax. Special luxury food and drink items accompany them and are often used to entertain other diplomats at a later time.

Diplomats also have free access to the diplomatic pouch that messengers carry across borders. Whereas custom officials check regular citizens' luggage when they travel from one nation to another, the pouch cannot be inspected. For the most part, only mail and small items are carried in the pouch.

Finally, foreign ambassadors have the right to be addressed as "Excellency." American diplomats, however, have changed this title to "The Honorable," feeling that "Excellency" sounds like a royal title. Nevertheless, in other countries, U.S. ambassadors are frequently addressed as "Excellency."

Not all diplomats in all countries have enjoyed equal privileges. Sometimes one country grants privileges to its visiting diplomats while its own representatives in another country do not have the same privileges. Today the U.S. State Department is working with other nations to be sure that certain privileges are the same for all foreign workers everywhere. Among these privileges are the freedom to travel throughout the host country and the right to own land in the host country.

An unexpected benefit of an ambassador's job sometimes occurs in the form of gifts. Historically, it was normal procedure for emissaries to bring gifts to the royal courts of foreign powers. It was always wise for a court to accept such gifts, since countries were often offended if their gifts were not accepted. Even in early Greek days, however, very expensive presents looked more like bribes.

Today, small token gifts like silver-framed photographs or pens are considered acceptable, while gifts of cars or jeweled medals are not. In 1957, King Saud of Saudi Arabia gave a $3,000 car—an expensive car in those days—to the U.S. State Department's Deputy

Chief of Protocol, Victor Purse. When Purse accepted the gift, he was reprimanded by his chief for poor judgment and was later transferred out of the Office of Protocol and into another division within the State Department.

In 1966, however, the U.S. Congress passed a law allowing diplomats to receive gifts of minimal value only. Such gifts include table favors, mementos, and inconsequential presents. When a substantial gift is given to a diplomat, the gift becomes the property of the United States. The receiver must then deposit it with the State Department. This agency then disposes of it according to law.

## Embassies as Sanctuaries

Not only diplomats have immunity. In fact, the entire embassy buildings and embassy grounds also have immunity. For many years it has been understood that when a government buys land in a foreign capital, the embassy grounds are considered the land of the country making the purchase. When the Philippines bought a building in Washington, D.C., for example, the embassy grounds and building became Philippine territory. This situation is called **extraterritoriality**.

Because they are extraterritorial, embassies have often been used as safe havens, or asylums, for ousted political leaders. Ordinarily embassies do not encourage asylum because it means interfering in the host country's business. Exceptions, however, have been made.

Perhaps the longest instance of asylum concerned a Hungarian priest, Cardinal József Mindszenty. During a Hungarian revolt in 1956, the cardinal was freed from political prison by a mob. He sought sanctuary in the U.S. legation in Budapest. Other Hungarian revolutionaries were given asylum in the Yugoslavian embassy in Budapest and were later promised safe conduct to travel to Yugoslavia. Once off Yugoslavian embassy grounds, however, they were seized, put in jail, and executed. Fearing similar treatment, Cardinal Mindszenty stayed in the U.S. legation for nearly fifteen years. He finally received special permission to leave safely and in 1971 took up residence in Rome.

In another instance, a Russian girl working as a maid in the U.S. embassy in Moscow became pregnant. As the time of birth approached, she did not want to leave the embassy. She thought that if the baby were born there, the child would automatically be an American citizen, since it was born on American soil. Local authorities would not interfere. Finally an embassy administrator hustled the mother-to-be into an ambulance, and she was taken to the hospital.

Even more recently, individuals have been using the sanctuary of embassies as a last resort to leave their own countries. Some climb the embassy fence to get inside, while others rush past the guards.

In 1978, seven Russians in Moscow tried to obtain emigration visas but were denied them by the Soviet government. As a consequence, the seven evaded Russian police and bolted past marines into the U.S. embassy compound. The fleeing Russians spent nearly five years in the basement of the embassy until Russian authorities in 1983 promised them safety and eventual emigration.

Very often the act of granting asylum to defectors means that the embassy is interfering in the host country's affairs. Therefore, embassy officials give sanctuary with caution. They are afraid that safe haven for defectors might set off a worldwide diplomatic crisis. It is one of the reasons that each year U.S. diplomatic posts turn down an estimated 150 requests for asylum.

Like Cardinal Mindszenty, citizens of a nation sometimes seek sanctuary in a foreign embassy in their own city. In a recent instance, embassy immunity worked in the opposite way: foreign citizens living in London remained in their own embassy for refuge.

Libyan exiles and students living in Britain did not like Col. Muammar el-Qaddafi, the man running their home country, or his government. The Libyan embassy in London, of course, was staffed with Qaddafi followers. Fearful that Qaddafi had secretly sent death squads to England to kill them, the students and exiles staged an anti-Qaddafi protest outside the Libyan embassy in April 1984. During the protest, shots were fired at them from the window of the Libyan embassy. Ten Libyan protesters were wounded, and a British policewoman was killed. Police, however, could not enter the embassy building or arrest the Qaddafi followers because both the building and its occupants were safe under the immunity law.

For 11 days there was a standoff between the Qaddafi

followers inside the building and the British police on the outside. Finally the Libyan government sent a plane for the embassy occupants, and the 30 Libyans inside the embassy received safe passage from the building to Heathrow Airport. They returned to Libya. The immunity law even extended to their luggage, which could not be searched when they left the country.

Because of this incident, Britain broke off diplomatic relations with Libya and brought home the British diplomats who had been posted in Tripoli, Libya's capital.

## Unwelcome Diplomats

When an ambassador or minister does offend the host country, the host can ask for the diplomat to be sent home. This can be done in one of two ways. First, the host nation can declare the diplomat **persona non grata**, which is Latin and means "a person not welcome." Or, a diplomat can be **handed his passports**, or dismissed without notice. Being handed your passports is a bit stronger than being declared persona non grata, but both mean about the same thing: go home.

Today, individuals can hold only one passport, but governments used to issue passports as exit visas, and a traveler might easily have more than one. The phrase "handed his passports" dates back to this time.

Dismissal from a country can stem from many causes—lawlessness, excessive traffic violations, or political changes. In October of 1952, George F. Kennan, then U.S. Ambassador to the Soviet Union, was termed persona non grata in the U.S.S.R. because of some remarks he made in public. While speaking to reporters at Tempelhof Airport in Berlin, Germany, about his Moscow embassy experience, he equated life in Moscow with that of a prisoner of war in Germany. Later the ambassador admitted that he had forgotten to make his remarks "off the record." When word got back to Soviet officials, Kennan was not allowed back into Russia. A U.S. airplane was sent to Moscow for Kennan's family and their belongings.

Not all unwelcome diplomats are ambassadors. During World War I, a German military attaché living in Washington, D.C. was suspected of plotting to destroy U.S. ammunition plants. He was declared persona non grata.

If a diplomat is declared persona non grata, he must go home. To stay would be useless, because the host country will not do business with him. His purpose for being in the foreign country will have vanished.

# 5
# The Rules of Diplomacy

**Protocol** is the term used to describe the rules and courtesies that govern diplomacy. Most of the rules that comprise protocol date back to 1814 and the Congress of Vienna. Surprisingly enough, they remain relevant today.

In 1928, the State Department formed the Office of Protocol to assist with receptions, official foreign visits, treatymaking, state funerals, and other formal occasions in which protocol is involved. Over the years the Office has expanded, and it now serves foreign diplomats as well as American ones, answering their questions about diplomatic immunity, privileges, and law.

Before a high-ranking diplomat travels to a foreign country to begin his job, certain protocol must be observed. The prospective ambassador, minister, or consul must receive permission from the foreign country to work there. Seldom is a diplomat rejected, but it is only wise and reasonable to clear him or her through the foreign government first before announcing the appointment.

In the mid-1700s, Sweden refused a British envoy because he had once visited a country with which Sweden was then at war. In 1984, the country of Guyana requested that President Reagan not appoint a prospective ambassador to its country. The man's name was withdrawn.

Upon a diplomat's actual arrival at his or her post, the minister of the host country is notified. In the U.S., this function belongs to the secretary of state. When the secretary of state has been notified of a new arrival, the State Department makes an appointment with the president to present his or her credentials, and the following scenario, set in Washington, is a typical one.

On the day of presentation, the new ambassador or diplomat dons an official business suit or his or her national dress. A U.S. protocol officer escorts the ambassador in a government car to the southwest entrance of the White House, which is the diplomatic entrance. The driveway is lined with an honor guard.

The U.S. chief of protocol meets the ambassador and escorts him or her to the Cabinet Room and then to the Oval Office, where the president stands between the U.S. and the presidential flags. The chief of protocol announces the ambassador, who presents his or her country's official credentials. After a few exchanges of papers and words, the chief of protocol and the ambassador retrace their route.

In other countries, credentials are presented in basically the same way. In London, ambassadors and their families are escorted to Buckingham Palace in coaches guided by scarlet-liveried drivers. The ceremony is longer when speeches must be interpreted, which is the case in most nations.

After individual credentials have been formally presented to a nation's head of state, the official automatically becomes a member of that nation's **diplomatic corps**. The diplomatic corps is made up of all the top-ranking diplomats posted to a particular country. In addition, it includes their secretaries, attachés, advisers, and families.

The diplomatic corps in Washington, D.C. has over 5,000 members. Four times a year, the U.S. produces a Diplomatic List, often referred to as the blue book. Within its pages are listed the countries in order of precedence, their embassies, their national holidays, and the members and spouses of their diplomatic staffs. Those listed enjoy full immunity under the law.

The diplomatic corps in each city has a **dean**. The dean is the foreign emissary who has been in the host country the longest. When, as in Washington, over 140 countries are represented by embassies, the top position holds a great deal of status. Though a foreign ambassador's tour of duty usually lasts for several years, deans often remain in their posts for an even longer time in order to hold the top rank for their countries.

Anatoly Dobrynin, the Soviet ambassador to the United States, was posted to the U.S. in March of 1962. He has been dean of the diplomatic corps in

Washington since 1979. Smaller countries of the world find particular prestige in having a dean of the diplomatic corps regardless of the country in which it is located.

In the past, it was the custom for new diplomats to call or visit other colleagues of higher rank at a new post. Today the large capitals are home to so many embassies that a new ambassador could not possibly adhere rigidly to this formality. Calling is still done, but leaving a calling card at an official's home is often sufficient and takes the place of a personal visit until such a meeting can be arranged. Sometimes small gatherings are arranged to take the place of both personal calls and calling cards.

In addition, the chief of protocol is responsible for informing all embassies of any new diplomats as they arrive in town. In this way they are introduced to the community, although it may be months before they actually meet many of their counterparts from other countries in person.

In many countries, the diplomatic corps is so large that there is not enough time for every diplomat to meet individually with every other diplomat. Large parties serve the purpose of bringing together these people so that they can get to know one another. The many lunches, dinners, teas, receptions, banquets, and parties enliven diplomatic life. Each of these events involves protocol. At an embassy dinner the host protocol officer may even post the seating arrangement outside the dining room so that the visitors know exactly where to sit.

An ambassador's official departure from a country is much more relaxed than his or her arrival. In the U.S., foreign diplomats ordinarily call on the secretary of state in Washington, D.C., and on other people with whom they may have worked closely. It is customary for departing ambassadors to give receptions for the diplomatic community and to be honored at ones given for them. They then return to their homelands and their successors take over.

# 6
# Diplomacy's Secret Side

Every nation has sensitive information that it wishes to keep secret from other countries and even sometimes from its own citizens. Embassies handle important economic, political, and military information. The staff of an embassy receives reports and sends messages to its head of state and to other countries. Some messages are so top-secret that diplomats must be sure no one sees them except the one person for whom the message is intended.

## Codes and Ciphers

There are several ways to send secret messages. One way is to use a code or cipher when writing the message. Ciphers rearrange letters or substitute signs or symbols (including letters, numbers, or words) for letters in a message so that it cannot be easily understood.

Persian secretaries in 500 A.D. used the names of birds for letters of the alphabet in their code. In the Morse Code, which is really a cipher, dashes and dots are used in place of each letter of the alphabet. An easy cipher might be one in which every letter in the alphabet was represented by the one preceding it (e.g. b by a, o by n, y by x). In this example, the word "boy" would be written "anx."

Codes differ from ciphers in that whole words or word groups are renamed or given symbols. "Call me on Saturday" might be encoded as "IBIT," while "Come over on Saturday" could be "IXIT." These are nonsense words that do not suggest the meanings of the phrases they represent in any way.

The problem with using codes, though, is that with enough time and effort, they can be cracked. For that reason, it is important to change codes frequently. Before long, it becomes difficult to devise a code not already used. Experienced codebreakers have no trouble cracking codes in different languages. Despite these drawbacks, codes are an important, economical way of keeping information and messages secret.

Not too many years ago, invisible inks also played a part in keeping diplomatic messages secret. Some chemical inks were disguised in perfumes, while others were written betweeen two halves of a split piece of paper. In both World War I and World War II, the Germans made frequent use of secret ink writing and developed this method into a fine art.

The Germans eventually came up with an even better method of passing along secret information and one that proved to be the focus of many spy movies. This innovation was the microdot, a photograph of a letter page reduced to the size of a typewriter period. In the early 1940s, a double agent tipped the Americans to watch for such dots. The first microdot was found more than a year later by a sharp-eyed technician who saw a glint on the outside of a suspicious envelope. When he looked more carefully, he found a tiny piece of film and peeled it off the envelope. It is hard to know how many times this method was used before it was detected.

## "Telebugging" and "Telescrambling"

The advent of the telephone as a common means of communication called for the development of two items: the "bug," a concealed listening device used to eavesdrop on conversations, and the scrambler, a machine used to protect conversations from being understood.

In 1945, the Russian government presented the U.S. ambassador's office in Moscow with an attractive large wooden eagle. The gift was given "in appreciation of American assistance" during World War II. Seven years later someone discovered that the wooden eagle was hollow and contained a bug.

**This handcarved wooden replica of the Great Seal of America, a gift of the Soviets, opens to reveal the space where the listening device was placed.**

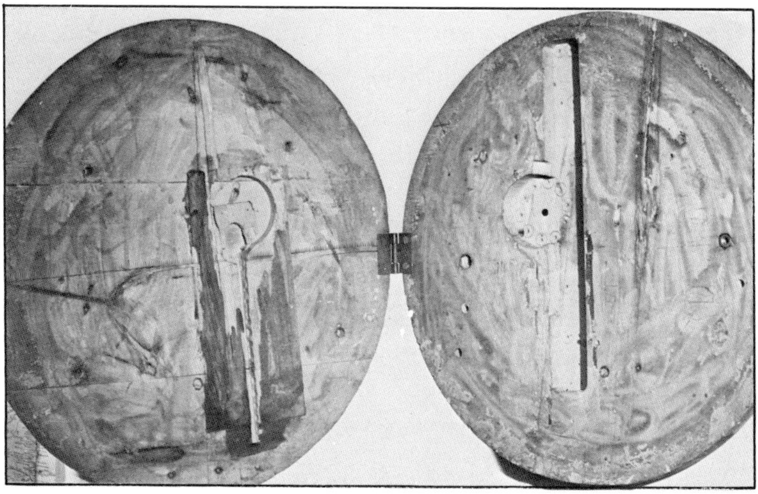

The scrambler is used primarily with telephones or radios. By shifting the frequencies of speech sounds, this machine scrambles ordinary words so that anyone listening in cannot understand the conversation. It sounds like gibberish. The telephone or radio on the receiving end is equipped with a descrambler which restores the words to their normal meaning.

During World War II, President Roosevelt often conferred via transatlantic telephone with the American ambassador in Paris and with Winston Churchill in England. Roosevelt preferred the telephone because of its swiftness and its personal contact. When such calls were made, elaborate scrambling measures were used through New York City.

The Germans, against whom the Allies were fighting, realized the significance of those phone conversations, and they put top priority on breaking the code used in the scrambling devices. They managed to do this within a few months, but took care to keep this fact a secret. They knew, of course, that when the news got back to the Allies, they would revert to coded telegraph communications. The Allies, however, soon replaced one scrambler system with another, and conversations were once again secure.

To protect top-secret reports and communications, all embassies have rooms where code materials are kept and where related work is done. Such areas are kept secure and off limits to all but a few people. Even misfortune cannot violate this security. One extreme example involved the Russian embassy in Ottawa, Canada, in 1956. Although a fire raced through the building, Russian officials, fearing the exposure of secret materials, would not allow Canadian firefighters on the grounds. Instead, the Russians insisted on removing all the papers. When firefighters were finally allowed into the burning building, it was too late. The fire had destroyed the embassy.

Today the United States is working to computerize secret documents in its foreign embassies. Each day, embassies in dangerous areas will store their classified materials in a data bank in Washington, D.C. If an embassy needs to recover any of the information, automatic coding facilities in Washington will allow the embassy to retrieve the information via satellite. This way, the State Department in Washington will have the classified information should its foreign embassy be threatened or destroyed.

## "None Swifter than These"

A common means of communication between embassies is by **courier**, or messenger. Official couriers carry pouches (in England they are called "bags" and in France, "valises") which contain mail and other light items. Perhaps one of the most effective code and courier networks was the Despacho Universal, which operated in Spain during the 1400s and 1500s. From this center, couriers left for all parts of the world at all times of the day and night. In the mid-1600s, the British established the first official diplomatic courier service. Since that time the pouch/

courier runs have served embassies all over the globe. Each country has its own courier system.

The first official American diplomatic courier was a captain of the brig *Dispatch*, bound for France in 1776. The military letters he carried were weighted so that in case of capture, they could be thrown overboard and would sink.

Until World War I, U.S. pouches were fastened by heavy wax seals. Most would be sent by regular mail or entrusted to an American traveling to the same destination. Many times a ship's captain or a naval officer would take them. Because pouches carried diplomatic data and were immune from search, there was a certain prestige about being selected as a courier.

Between the years of 1919 and 1945, the United States established and abandoned official courier services several times. When necessary, the pouches were carried by military personnel. In 1946, the United States instituted the system of worldwide schedules that is in effect today. The safety of diplomatic pouches has been absolute: in the U.S. service, no letter or pouch has ever been stolen from a diplomatic courier.

During the 1950s, the Russians added another safety feature to their pouches. They sent messages or reports on undeveloped film in their bags. If the pouch was opened by someone other than the person who was supposed to open it, the film would automatically be exposed and ruined. The messages themselves would remain safe.

**A State Department employee with a diplomatic pouch**

U.S.A.
DEPARTMENT OF STATE
DIPLOMATIC POUCH
X6-154

The U.S. courier network runs like a giant relay service. One courier delivers large padlocked mail pouches—as many as twenty-five on an average run—to one destination. Other couriers carry on from there, each going in a different direction. Couriers never know the contents of the pouches they carry and must never leave them unattended.

Today's United States Diplomatic Courier Service, with its motto "None swifter than these," numbers close to seventy-five couriers.

# 7

# Working in the Foreign Service

No matter where on the globe you live, employment in the foreign service has its advantages and disadvantages. While it provides adventure and often excitement to those who choose it, it can also be a nomadic existence. Foreign service workers no sooner become settled into a new country and begin to learn its ways than they are moved on to another post.

About 7,500 United States citizens work throughout the world in the Foreign Service. The experience and education a person needs to enter the Foreign Service is directly related to the level at which he or she wants to work.

## Kinds of Jobs

There are many different kinds of jobs in the foreign

service. **Foreign service specialists** bring their own kinds of expertise to the job, whether as librarians, secretaries, doctors, nurses, medical technicians, or English teachers.

Those candidates who become **foreign service officers** can be assigned to administrative, consular, economic, or political duties. Since 1980, candidates for the foreign service who demonstrate skill or experience in business are considered for a position as a **foreign commercial service officer** in cooperation with the Department of Commerce. These people work with governments and individuals to promote American businesses in other countries.

Another area which attracts applicants is USIA, the United States Information Agency. This independent agency oversees the operation of the Voice of America, the global radio network of the U.S. government. Those USIA staff members who work for the Voice of America do so in the U.S., producing media materials for overseas use. USIA also employs foreign service officers who carry out communications work overseas, either as information officers or cultural officers.

Among their other duties, information officers set up press conferences, publicize embassy events, and aid American journalists who are visiting their host country. The job of the cultural affairs officer is to encourage cultural and educational exchanges between the host country and the U.S. This includes such tasks as arranging for an American singer to perform in the host country or helping to set up a student exchange program.

## Applying for the Foreign Service

Top-level diplomats, such as ambassadors and ministers, achieve their posts either through appointment or after years of foreign service experience.

Both foreign service specialists and foreign service officers must meet certain qualifications before they can even apply. They must be U.S. citizens and able to pass a thorough background security investigation. They must also meet certain medical standards and be free to relocate anywhere in the world. Those applying to be foreign service specialists must be 21 years old, while those applying to be foreign service officers must be at least 20.

Most nations demand top performance for those entering the foreign service at the senior level. France requires extremely difficult oral and written examinations along with extensive knowledge of other countries. West German exams are not as difficult, but candidates who are accepted are put on a long probationary period. British applicants are not only exposed to grueling oral and written tests, but must also pass a series of difficult weekend tests where they are confronted with problems to solve. Many candidates are washed out during these filtering processes.

The United States requires different examinations for different jobs. Those applying to be foreign service specialists may be tested in their area of specialization or may just need to prove that they have the required experience and degree.

Those applying to be foreign service officers must

take a written examination. Below are two samples of the kind of questions on the test. Most of the questions are even more difficult than these two.

1. If each of the following groups of artists could collaborate on a work, which group most probably would create an American folk opera based upon themes drawn from the early history of the nation?

a. Leonard Bernstein, Jack Kerouac, and Pearl Primus
b. Aaron Copland, Carl Sandburg, and Agnes de Mille
c. Lukas Foss, Ernest Hemingway, and George Balanchine
d. Paul Hindemith, Henry Miller, and Anthony Tudor
e. Gian-Carlo Menotti, Tennessee Williams, and Martha Graham

2. In recent decades the composition of the population of Japan has been changed primarily by which of the following:

a. Emigration planned and directed by the government
b. The accelerated rate of industrialization since the Second World War
c. An increase in life expectancy
d. The restriction of immigration
e. The drastic reduction of the birthrate

It is unlikely that you answered both questions correctly. (The answers are 1-b and 2-e.) Like these examples, the questions are drawn from all fields of study including history, literature, political science, law, economics, government, and international relations. By the time a candidate has graduated from college, he or she will have had courses in many of these subjects and the questions will not seem so unfamiliar.

The written test is just one part of the screening process a Foreign Service applicant must go through.

Other kinds of examinations and interviews are designed to assess the applicant's decision-making and problem-solving skills, leadership potential, and social skills. Successful applicants must demonstrate a complete command of the English language, both in written and spoken form.

Because the Foreign Service is trying to present a realistic picture of the United States, it wishes to attract people from all walks of life. Special programs have been established to recruit people of different ethnic groups, religions, educational levels, and work backgrounds.

## On the Job

Once a person has been accepted by the Foreign Service, he or she goes through several weeks of basic orientation. Language training, if necessary, can take up to 24 additional months. When all training is complete, the new foreign service employee is assigned to a post overseas or to a job in Washington, D.C.

For those going overseas on diplomatic work, the

United States Foreign Service Institute provides an assignment notebook, which gives information on health issues, how to pack, mail, pets, insurance, foreign clothes sizes, employment opportunities for other members of the family, time conversions, income tax, and other concerns.

The length of service varies from post to post. Appointments last from two to four years and can extend to five years depending on the job. The government pays for travel to and from a duty post, and also provides medical insurance, a housing allowance, home and sick leave, and retirement pay. Educational allowances are sometimes granted, as are provisions and allowances for family members.

The Department of State, which oversees the foreign service for America, employs approximately 25,000 people. About 7,500 work in the United States, 7,500 work overseas in the foreign service, and the remaining 10,000 are foreign employees who work in U.S. embassies and consulates in the host countries.

A typical fair-sized embassy in South America might have a staff of close to 100 foreign service officers, not including military personnel. These positions would include several economic officers, a disbursing officer, a telecommunications specialist, a sociologist, a general engineer, a Peace Corps representative, more than one physician, and an assistant agricultural attaché. This staff would be supported by many clerical and technical workers, both from the U.S. and South America. In all, the actual embassy employment would amount to almost 225 persons.

## Internships

Perhaps the best way to get a taste of what the Foreign Service is really like is to work in it for a while. Each year, the Service offers a limited number of paid internships to junior, senior, and graduate level college students whose studies relate directly to the work done by the foreign service. Most jobs are located in Washington, D.C. Typical projects might involve assisting in law cases, conducting research, working in computer science, drafting correspondence, or selecting topics for speeches.

USIA also offers two kinds of internships. One internship is with the Voice of America and the other is as a summer guide for USIA exhibits in foreign countries.

When thinking of any job as a possible career, it is a good idea to consider it from all angles. For instance, not all of the foreign posts are in glamorous cities like London and Paris. Some are very small and out of the way, where plumbing and electricity are not always reliable. Some involve harsh climates, and some may present security risks.

On the other hand, the Service offers a first-hand look at another culture and the opportunity to travel. People who work in the Foreign Service also have a chance to be truly useful—to serve their own country as well as people in their host countries.

Each individual has his or her own reason for joining the Foreign Service. American Marguerite King, a veteran of five different assignments, gives her reason:

"The Foreign Service isn't for everybody, but some of what we do can foster peace instead of war. What can top that?"

For more information about entering the Foreign Service, write to:

Foreign Service Officer
Recruitment Branch
Box 9317
Rosslyn Station
Arlington, VA 22209-0317

Information about internships is available from:

Paid Summer Intern Program
Special Recruitment Branch
U.S. Department of State
Washington, DC 20520

Voice of America Internship Program
U.S. Information Agency
400 C Street, SW
Washington, DC 20547

Exhibit Guide Internship Program
Employment Branch
U.S. Information Agency
400 C Street, SW
Washington, DC 20547

# 8
# The Many Kinds of Diplomacy

Diplomacy has come a long way since the roaming ambassadors of the Greek Age. Innovations in communications and travel have changed the way in which diplomacy can take place. A transatlantic trip which took fifteen days by ship in 1830 and ten hours by air in 1950 today takes three and a half hours by Concorde. Thanks to the jet, heads of state can now meet on a personal level in a matter of hours.

## Summit Diplomacy

During the past ten years, heads of state for seven of the world's industrial countries (France, Britain, West Germany, Italy, Canada, Japan, and the U.S.) have met annually to try to settle economic problems. At these Big Seven meetings, leaders discuss the effect of such financial issues as interest rates, trade, and currency on business between their nations. They attempt, not always successfully, to find solutions to their problems.

Since the development of nuclear weapons over forty years ago, arms build-up has been a growing global concern. SALT I (Strategic Arms Limitation Talks of 1969) and SALT II (1979) were conferences that addressed the issue of restricting nuclear arms. America was represented at both meetings by Ambassadors-at-Large, special diplomats employed to handle delicate negotiations.

In 1985, U.S. Secretary of State George Schultz and Soviet Foreign Minister Andrei Gromyko discussed the same subject again, this time including missile defense systems as well as nuclear weapons.

The North Atlantic Treaty Organization (NATO) is another group that deals in global diplomacy. The organization is made up of North American and European countries that handle regional environmental and defense problems of member nations. England's Prime Minister Margaret Thatcher called on ships, planes, and soldiers from the NATO agency to help in the victory against Argentina during the Falkland Islands crisis in 1982.

**Summit diplomacy**, or meetings between heads of state and top diplomats, will never replace the continual diplomacy conducted by embassy staff. While it is important for heads of state to meet, quite often the meetings are too short for differences to be resolved or too public for decisions to be made on the spot. Nixon's landmark visit to China in 1972 opened the door between China and the U.S., but it was five years before full diplomatic relations were established between the two countries.

## Expert and Individual Diplomacy

While the planet earth has remained the same size, the population inhabiting it has almost tripled since 1900. This population explosion is the cause of many global problems, including world hunger, air and water pollution, and depletion of natural resources.

Many international governmental and non-governmental agencies, some part of the United Nations, are hard at work on these problems. In addition to strictly governmental agencies, business and religious organizations also help further world understanding and relieve world suffering.

Although the United States and the Soviet Union have had serious periods of strain since 1958, cultural exchange between the two countries has survived and continued. Musical groups, lecturers, scientists, and athletes have all been informal diplomats, contributing their talents to promote world understanding. Statesmen believe that the U.S. ping-pong team sent to China in 1971 was partially responsible for opening relations with that country so that Nixon could visit the following year.

In 1983, Congressman Morris Udall proposed a U.S.-Soviet Student Exchange for Peace Program. This proposal outlines a plan for exchanging 2,000 young people from each country for a year of work and study. The young people, ranging in age from 15 to 20, are to be drawn from a variety of backgrounds. Udall points to the program as "diplomacy in human terms."

Teacher and student exchanges have long promoted understanding between cultures. Over the past thirty years, the Youth for Understanding organization has been responsible for the exchange of more than 100,000 teenagers between 23 countries. Other active organizations include the International Christian Youth Exchange, the American Scandinavian Student Exchange, and exchanges sponsored by international Rotary and Lions clubs. Other nations, too, support such programs.

Education is only one of the fields in which contributions have been made. Valeria Boyer was considered a "shirt-sleeves ambassador" in 1969 when she traveled to Athens, Greece, to help set up a small hospital using her managerial skills. Ms. Boyer was one of the many volunteers of the International Executive Service Corps, a group of experienced U.S. executives who share their technical and managerial skills with businesses or institutions in developing countries. IESC, a group sponsored by the U.S. government and U.S. corporations, has completed more than 8,500 assignments in 72 countries since 1964. In doing her overseas job so well and in such a respected manner, Ms. Boyer practiced diplomacy in a quiet, effective way.

Foreign embassies help make all these programs work. They also make sure that U.S. agencies abroad act in line with U.S. policies. First-hand knowledge of a nation and personal diplomatic contact cannot be replaced.

Whatever form it takes, diplomacy is the give-and-take, softsell approach to peace, much more effective than a club on the head or a bomb devastating everything. Travel and technology have brought the countries of the world, no matter how many miles apart, close to each other and made them interdependent upon one another. Today, what touches one nation touches all.

**These workers are checking a soybean field in the Dominican Republic. The United Nations Development Program is helping the country increase its food production.**

# Glossary of Terms

**ambassador:** specifically, a diplomatic agent of the highest rank; generally, any representative or messenger

**chancery:** the office of an embassy

**chargé d'affaires:** a diplomat who substitutes for an ambassador or minister in his or her absence

**chief of mission:** the director of an embassy (usually an ambassador, a minister, or a chargé d'affaires)

**consul:** an official residing in a foreign land to represent commercial and other interests of his or her home country

**consul general:** a consul of the first rank having jurisdiction in several places or over several consuls

**consulate:** the residence and office of a consul

**country team:** the group of people, including agency representatives and other senior advisors, that reports to an ambassador in a foreign nation

**courier:** specifically, a member of the U.S. Diplomatic Courier Service entrusted with carrying messages; generally, any messenger

**dean:** the senior member and spokesperson of a diplomatic corps in a capital city

**delegation:** a group of people chosen to represent others

**deputy chief of mission:** the diplomat second in command to the ambassador at an embassy

**diplomacy:** the art and skill of handling affairs without fighting

**diplomat:** a person skilled in handling affairs between nations and people in a peaceful manner

**diplomatic corps:** all of the diplomats present in a capital city taken as a whole

**diplomatic mission:** an embassy, legation, or consulate in a foreign country

**embassy:** the official office of an ambassador in a foreign country

**emissary:** a diplomatic person sent on a mission

**envoy:** a person delegated to represent one government in its dealings with another government

**extraterritoriality:** exemption of embassy grounds and buildings from the jurisdiction of local laws

**foreign commercial service officers:** career officers of the Department of Commerce who help American business people with foreign trade

**foreign service officers:** career officers of the Department of State or the U.S. Information Agency who work either in the home country or overseas

**foreign service specialists:** foreign service workers such as secretaries, communications officers, engineers, or nurses, who support diplomatic, consular, commercial, and other services overseas

**handed one's passports:** to be dismissed immediately by a host country as a diplomat and told to return home

**immunity:** exemption of foreign diplomatic agents from local and national laws

**legation:** an official residence and office of a diplomatic minister in a foreign country

**minister:** a diplomatic agent ranked below an ambassador

**nuncio:** an ambassador from the Vatican in Rome

**persona non grata:** one who is not welcome in a particular country

**precedence:** the ranking order of importance

**protocol:** the rules and courtesies of diplomatic life

**right of chapel:** a privilege which allows ambassadors to arrange religious services of their own faith in countries where it would not be permitted otherwise

**summit diplomacy:** world or bilateral meetings between heads of state for the purpose of solving international problems peacefully

# A Gallery of Diplomats

## Robert R. Livingston (1746-1813)

Active in politics in his home state of New York, Livingston was appointed in 1781 as the first Secretary of Foreign Affairs for the new country of America. Later this office, which manages foreign matters, became the Department of State.

As minister to France in the early 1800s, Livingston helped to arrange for the Louisiana Purchase. This additional territory comprises more than one-fifth of the total United States lands today.

## William Palfrey (?-1780)

Not usually dangerous, foreign service work has nevertheless resulted in loss of human life on occasion, more frequently since embassies have become targets for terrorist groups.

Massachusetts-born Palfrey was the first American consul and was also the first person in the U.S. Foreign Service to lose his life in the line of duty. While he was en route to France as consul in 1780, his ship was lost at sea.

## **John Quincy Adams** (1767-1848)

Diplomacy was not new to Adams. Even as a boy, he often accompanied his famous father, President John Adams, overseas. Not long after America declared itself a new nation, the young Adams traveled to Prussia as minister. The German officer on duty in Berlin would not accept Adam's letter of authority and did not allow him into Berlin. The reason given by the German officer was that there was no such country as the United States of America!

## **James Buchanan** (1791-1868)

Born in a log cabin in Pennsylvania, James Buchanan learned early to appreciate the simple things in life. Before becoming the fifteenth president of the United States, he ran into dress problems while a minister to Great Britain in 1853. The U.S. secretary of state had advised diplomats to wear the simple clothes of a U.S. citizen at functions in other countries. Buchanan agreed with this plan, but Queen Victoria and London society were shocked. They required fancy dress at court occasions. Finally, however, the Queen relented. She allowed Buchanan the simple clothes but asked that he wear a small sword to distinguish him from the court servants.

## **Pierre Soule** (1801-1870)

Not all diplomats have proven tactful. Soule, a

Frenchman naturalized in the U.S., was aggressive and impulsive. Sent as a minister to Spain in 1853, he talked outspokenly of obtaining Cuba as an American territory—an unpopular issue with the Spanish. To make matters worse, while assigned there, Soule fought a duel with a French official to avenge supposed insults to Soule's wife and lamed the man for life. After other stormy encounters with European diplomats, Soule resigned and returned to the United States.

**Frederick Douglass** (1817-1895)

Douglass was raised in Maryland as a slave, but escaped bondage and was later freed. An intelligent and courageous man, he lectured and wrote for anti-slavery groups. He was eventually appointed as minister to Haiti in 1889, becoming one of the first blacks in America to hold a diplomatic post.

**Wilbur J. Carr** (1870-1942)

Career officer Carr, a farm boy from Ohio, is known as the "Father of the Foreign Service." Strangely enough, he spent most of his forty-five-year career on the job in Washington, D.C., and did not receive a foreign post until he was sixty-seven years old. Just before World War II, he was appointed as ambassador to Czechoslavakia.

During Carr's many years in Washington, D.C., he helped turn the consular corps into an efficient and

William Palfrey

Pierre Soule

Frederick Douglass

Wilbur J. Carr

Ruth Bryan Owen

John Foster Dulles

William C. Bullitt

Clifton R. Wharton

professional organization. Later, with others, he was instrumental in unifying the consular and the diplomatic sections into one service under the Rogers Act of 1924.

**Ruth Bryan (Owen) Rohde** (1885-1954)

Illinois-born Ruth Bryan, daughter of William Jennings Bryan, was reared in a family well-acquainted with both travel and politics. After careers in nursing, teaching, and politics, she was appointed minister to Denmark in 1933. With this appointment, Bryan became the first woman to head a U.S. diplomatic mission.

**John Foster Dulles** (1888-1959)

Born in the nation's capital, Dulles had a natural background for a career in diplomacy. As a lawyer, he served as counsel and advisor to many international conferences over a period of fifty-two years.

He was, in his time, the most widely traveled secretary of state. During his six years in that office, he logged nearly 560,000 air miles. Such a distance would be like encircling the earth 22 times. Dean Rusk later topped this mark, but it took him two additional years to do it.

**Robert O. Yardley** (1889-1958)

Indiana-born Yardley was one of the most efficient

codebreakers in U.S. history. He gathered linguists around him for diplomatic and intelligence work and set up offices especially to deal with different types of codes. When a blank paper found in a woman's shoe heel turned out to be a message in secret ink, it sparked the establishment of a secret ink section. Likewise, coded messages in German shorthand caused the department to set up a shorthand section.

Yardley's career was cut short in 1929, however, when new Secretary of State Henry Stimson took over and closed down the codebreaking operations. The reason, Stimson was reported as saying, was that gentlemen did not read each other's mail.

## **William C. Bullitt** (1891-1967)

Pennsylvanian by birth, Bullitt joined the State Department after World War I and worked on and off in diplomatic affairs. He was the first U.S. ambassador to the Soviet Union. During World War II, he served as ambassador-at-large and kept President Roosevelt informed (through coded messages) of affairs in France. Before the end of the war, Bullitt left U.S. government service to fight with the French army.

## **Frances E. Willis** (1899-)

Frances Willis, born in Illinois, chose the Foreign Service as a career. When she was appointed ambassador to Switzerland in 1953, she became the first woman Foreign Service officer to attain that rank.

At one point in her career, she used the principle of extraterritoriality for her own safety. With world War II coming on, Frances Willis and fellow Foreign Service staff members took refuge in the American legation in Brussels where they worked. For two months they were cut off from all contact with the outside world until arrangements could be made for their safe passage from Belgium.

## **Clifton R. Wharton** (1899-)

The stiff entrance requirements of the foreign service, including the educational qualifications and the difficult exam, have discouraged many people from even applying. But Clifton R. Wharton was not stopped by these hurdles, nor by the discrimination he felt as a black. After earning a law degree and becoming a law clerk for the State Department, Wharton took the foreign service test and passed in 1925. He subsequently served in several missions in Africa and Europe. As minister to Rumania in 1958, Wharton became the first black to head a U.S. delegation to a European country. He finished his career as ambassador to Norway in the early 1960s.

## **George F. Kennan** (1904-)

Like working his way up in a business firm, Wisconsin-born George Kennan began his diplomatic career by joining the Foreign Service one year out of college. He spent time in Europe in different diplomatic jobs.

When World War II broke out, he was caught in Germany and spent several months in a prisoner-of-war camp. In 1952, Kennan was appointed ambassador to Russia and later became ambassador to Yugoslavia.

## John Kenneth Galbraith (1908-)

Not all diplomats work in the Foreign Service before becoming ambassadors. John Kenneth Galbraith was born in Canada but later became a U.S. citizen. A man interested in ecomomics and politics, he is both author and educator. In 1961 President Kennedy put Galbraith's specialized knowledge and diplomatic skills to use for the nation by appointing him ambassador to India.

## Park Fields Wollam (1917-)

During an uprising that led to the Cuban revolution, Cuban rebels kidnapped Americans from a nickel company in Moa Bay, Cuba. U.S. Consul Park Wollam, posted close to Moa Bay, risked his life by going up into the hills unarmed to meet guerrilla leaders. Over a period of five weeks, while constantly under guard, Wollam spoke for the hostages' release. Without the power to recognize the rebel government and without granting them serious advantages, Wollam persuaded the rebels to free the captives. Eventually all hostages were evacuated by helicopter. Wollam was the last American to go.

Jeane Kirkpatrick

John Kenneth Galbraith

Bruce Laingen

Henry Kissinger

## Henry Alfred Kissinger (1923-)

Author, teacher, and diplomat, Henry Kissinger served in several government offices before becoming U.S. Secretary of State. German by birth, Kissinger came to the U.S. in 1938 and became a citizen five years later. Besides arranging agreements between countries involved in the Arab-Israeli War, Kissinger helped negotiate an end to the conflict in Vietnam. For his work in that cease-fire, he won the Nobel Peace Prize in 1973.

## Jeane Kirkpatrick (1926-)

Jeane Kirkpatrick's speeches reflect the plain-spoken frankness of her midwestern birth. She was named permanent U.S. ambassador to the United Nations in New York in 1980, a post she held for four years.

## L. Bruce Laingen (1922-)

Minnesota-born L. Bruce Laingen was caught in Tehran, Iran, during the Iranian hostage crisis in 1979. He and fifty-one other Americans were held hostage for fourteen months in the U.S. embassy. Though captive rather than chief, Laingen, as chargé d'affaires, was ranking officer for the Americans. All were released in January 1981.

# Index